V RD, C M & THE CHEVIOTS

by **FRANK GRAHAM**

1982

I.S.B.N. 0 85983 066 7

Published by FRANK GRAHAM
6 Queen's Terrace, Newcastle upon Tyne, NE2 2PL

Printed by Howe Brothers (Gateshead) Ltd.

CONTENTS

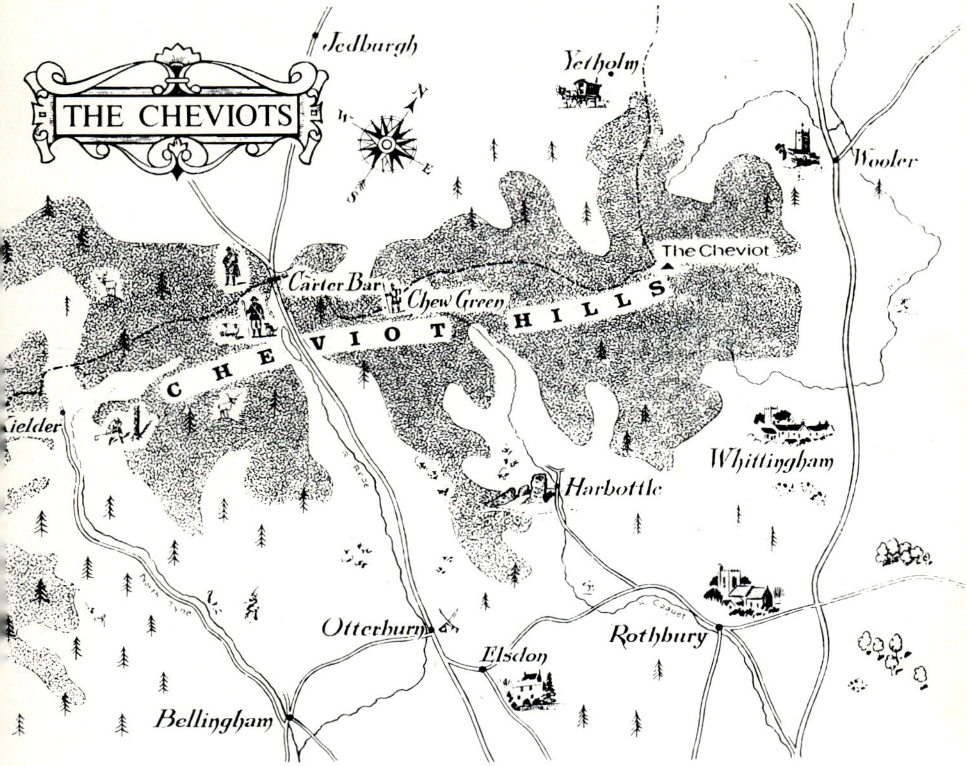

THE CHEVIOTS

Let our pilgrim footsteps seek
Old Cheviot's pathless mossy peak;
For there the mountain spirit still
Lingers around the lonely hill.

Thomas Pringle

The Cheviots emerged some 350 million years ago. Mighty volcanoes and volcanic eruptions threw up lava and ash to a height of thousands of feet. Over the centuries the huge mass was worn down into the rounded grassy hills we know today. The harder granitic rocks formed the higher hill tops occupying about 25 square miles of the central Cheviots including the Cheviot (2,676 feet), Cair Hill (2,545 feet), Hedgehope (2,348 feet), Comb Hill (2,132 feet), and Middleton Crags (1,324 feet).

Many milleniums later a mighty river flowing from the north deposited huge quantities of sand which formed the red sandstone of the Chillingham ridge. Between the Chillingham ridge and Cheviot lies Milfield Plain. It covers about 12 square miles and consists of deposits of sand, clay and gravel laid down when the site was a great lake at the end of the glacial period.

The sour soils of the Cheviot fell tops are favourable to the growth of blaeberry, cloudberry and moor-grass, although the vegetation has changed over the centuries. In former times the area was described as the *great forest of Cheviot* where herds of deer roamed. In the 16th century a little was still left and a contemporary description says there were "many allers and other ramell wood, the grounde was overgrown with linge, and some with moss, but still there was great plenty of red-deer and roes".

In the Survey of Waste Lands, 1542, we are told "the Scottes as well by nighte time secretly, as upon the daie tyme with more force, do come into the said forrest of Chevyott dyverse tymes and steale and carry awaie much of the saide wood, which ys to them a great proffyte for the mayntenance of their houses and buyldinges, and small redresse can be had by the lawes and customes of the marches".

The Cheviots form a natural barrier between England and Scotland covering some 200 square miles of Northumberland and 100 of Roxburghshire. They have a character all their own and from their summits fine views can be obtained. George Tait wrote many years ago. "On a bright summer day I enjoyed from one of the spurs of the Cheviots a magnificent view over part of the range. During the morning the tops of the hills had been wreathed in mist, but towards the afternoon, while looking down the deep valley of the College, and tracing the headlong course of the river among the rocks, a light breeze sprung up and rolled away the mist from one of the hill-tops, and then from others in succession, until the sun lighted up, with marvellous brilliancy, the whole of the mountains. Great pillared rocks appeared, and long trains of purple stones blended their tints with bright green herbage; crags crested the summit's, or broke out of the sides of some of the hills, resembling ruined towers and castles, and the hills and valleys rolling into each other appeared to rise and fall like the billows of a great ocean".

The Cheviots are rich in ancient earthworks, iron age forts and dwellings of the Votadini who inhabited Northumberland before the Romans came. At that time the weather was cool and damp with mild winters which made the area more suitable for settlement. Their characteristic type of hut dwellings survived well into the Middle Ages being similar to the shepherd's *shielings* of a later date.

The Cheviots have their share of legends. A party of hunters when chasing a roe near the Henhole were lured into a cleft in the rocks by the sweetest music they had ever heard. They were never seen again. The best known story is told in the ballad called *Black Adam of Cheviot* published by Fred Sheldon in the *Minstrelsy of the English Border*.

The poem tells how Black Adam a noted freebooter, also called the "Rider of Cheviot", burst into a wedding party at Wooperton, robbing the women of their jewelry and after raping the bride stabbed her to death. The bridegroom, one Wight Fletcher, who had been away seeking the priest, returned just in time to hear "Black Adam's laugh o' scorn". Taking his bride's kerchief, which was all stained with blood, Wight Fletcher went in pursuit of the freebooter. A terrible chase ensued. The riever reached Henhole and with a desperate leap of more than seven yards gained his lair which was a cave in a high cliff. Then

"He held a stane in baith his hondes,
And swore so save his sowl,
If Fletcher lap, to gar his bodie
Into the stream to roll.

'Ise try your brag, ye mean caytiff,'
Quo' Fletcher, and lap the sheugh;
Black Adam wi' ane heavy pash,
Bluid frae his forehead drew.

The blow it struck him off his feet,
Or ere he gained the bank;
He gave Black Adam a ghastly paik,
And back Wight Fletcher sank.

But as he slippit oure the edge,
He clutched at his enemie,
And hung oure yonder fearful steep,
Wi' ae grip o' Adam's knee.

'Unloose thy gripe, thou Wight Fletcher,
And I will spare thy life;'
The youth smiled grimly on his foe,
A warsling in the strife.

They tottered on the varra brink
O' that precipice so high;
Black Adam clung unto a rock,
For he feared sic death to die.

And now their scowling een were close,
And they fand each ither's breath;
And every struggle Black Adam gave
Was nearer till his death.

The rock it slippit frae Adam's clutch,
As he wrenchit bane and limb;
Fingers o' iron and nerves o' steel
Wight Fletcher kept on him.

Loud and lang Black Adam shrieked,
    But naething Fletcher said;
And there was neither twig or branch
    Upon their rocky bed.

Slowly right owre then they fell,
    For Fletcher his hold did keep;
A minute and their twa bodies
    Went crashing doune the steep.

There was a splash as the waters flew
    Half up the rugged dell;
The torrent rushed and the water gushed,
    But a' was dethely still."

One of the first tourists to climb Cheviot was Daniel Defoe in 1728. He had the assistance of a guide and "five or six country boys and young fellows". In his *Tour through Great Britain* he writes: "As we mounted higher we found the hill steeper than at first, also our horses began to complain, and draw their haunches up heavily, so we went very softly. However, we mov'd still, and went on till the height began to look really frightful, for I must own, I wished myself down again . . . We were the more uneasy about mounting higher, because we all had a notion that when we came to the top we should be just as upon a pinnacle, that the hill narrowed to a point, and we should have only room enough to stand, with a precipice every way round us; and with these apprehensions we all sat down upon the ground and said we would go no further. When, however, our guide perceived our mistake, he assured us there was room enough on the top of the hill to run a race if we thought fit, and we need not fear anything of being blown off the precipice as we had suggested; so, he encouraging us, we went on and reach't the top of the hill in about half-an-hour more".

There are three routes by which Cheviot can be climbed. The one usually chosen is by way of Earle, Middleton Hall and Langleeford.* As far as Langleeford farm there is a good motor road.

From here the tourist climbs the hill in a north-westerly direction. The distance is about three miles but the going is heavy. Cheviot top is a flat summit of some 50 acres. It consists of bogs and stagnant pools some of which are occasionally frozen at mid-summer. The highest points are marked by heaps of stones called the eastern and western cairns.

A second route from Wooler leads us over the Kettles and across Wooler Common having Earle Hill Head on the left (south). Westward is Hartheugh, with its fine steeps of blue glidders and two crested summit. The path we follow is now called Hell-path and the slopes down to the Common Burn are called the Devil's Knowe. To the north is Watch Hill (1,126 feet) whose rocky eminence was probably

**Hedgehope and Cheviot are pleasant bits of ground,*
But such a place as Langleeford is rarely to be found.

used as an outlook post in former times. Stretching north from it is Fredden Hill (Trodden Gares) whose western ravine is called Whisky Cleugh because of its use in smuggling days. Broadstruther lies in front of us. From there two miles further on is Goldscleugh, the point from which the ascent is made.

The third route is by way of Kirknewton and Hethpool up the magnificent glen of the College Burn. Above the burn are the remains of the prehistoric hill-forts of Great Hetha, Whitehall and Hethpool Bell. The beauties of the College Burn reach a climax in the wild and picturesque chasm called the *Henhole*. Black crags on each side rise precipitously to a height of 250 feet on whose inaccessible ledges nest the raven and peregrine falcon. Sunshine never enters the depth of Henhole; so often in the middle of summer a small patch of snow, called the *Snow Egg* is found here*. The rocky peak above Henhole is crowned by Auchhope Cairn (2,382 feet). Half a mile to the south of the cairn is a grassy mound (2,419 feet) marking the highest point on the Border line. Near by is a fractured outcrop of rock about 17 feet high called the *Hanging Stone*. It derives its names from the circumstance of a packman being strangled by his pack slipping over the edge and tightening the strap round his neck. What a packman was doing up here is a mystery. This stone formed the boundary between the East and Middle Marches. Another cairn on the border is called the Schil (1,985 feet). It may be a Bronze Age burial mound since it consists of a huge heap of stones.

Hedgehope (2,348 feet) is the second highest of the Cheviot range. Between it and the neighbouring Standrop Rigg is a syke near which a Highlander named "Black Rory" had his whisky still early in the 19th century. A green spot near it is called *Rory's Gair*; the word *gair* being a small strip of green ground among heather and ferns.

At the foot of Hedgehope, to the east, standing on peaty ground on the moor by *Threestoneburn* is a stone circle consisting of thirteen red stones in an oval of 340 feet circumference, but only five are upright. Megalithic remains are uncommon in Northumberland but several rude stone monuments such as these are found in the Cheviot area.

* *In a bank of clay near Henhole were found some massive mountings of cast bronze harness and horse-trappings of the late Celtic period.*

WOOLER

Wooler is a quiet small rural town situated on a slope above the Wooler water. It is a health and holiday resort and the best base for visits to the Cheviot Hills. Wooler formed one of the ancient baronies into which Northumberland was divided after the Norman Conquest. Henry I granted it to Robert de Muschampe, a family long since extinct. At that time Wooler was probably a waste and the building of the castle may have provided a nucleus around which the village grew.

It became an early centre of the woollen industry and so in the 13th century was one of the richest townships of Northumberland. The town was almost destroyed by fire in 1722, and again, in 1862. There are therefore no buildings of historic importance left. The church was rebuilt in 1863 after the fire. In the 16th century it had been a dilapidated thatched building but was rebuilt in 1763. Although most of Wooler is early 19th century the unadorned stone public buildings and cottages form an attractive and harmonious village.

Wooler has long been famous as a health resort. In 1791 Sir Walter Scott came here. In a letter he gives an account of his stay at a farmhouse outside the town "Behold a letter from the mountain, for I am very snugly settled here in a farmer's house, about six miles from Wooler, in the very centre of the Cheviot Hills, in one of the wildest and most romantic situations . . . To add to my satisfaction we are amidst places renowned by the feats of former days; each hill is crowned with a tower, or camp, or cairn; and in no situation can you be nearer more fields of battle . . . Out of the brooks with which these hills are intersected, we pull trouts of half-a-yard in length and we are in the very country of muir-fowl. My uncle drinks the goat's whey here, as I do ever since I understood it was brought to his bedside every morning at six by a very pretty dairy-maid. All the day we shoot, fish, walk and ride; dine and sup on fish struggling from the steam, and the most delicious heath-fed mutton, barn-door fowls, pays (pies), milk-cheese, etc, all in perfection; and so much simplicity resides among these hills that a pen, which could write at least, was not to be found about the house, though belonging to a considerable farmer, till I shot the crow with whose quill I write this epistle".

Wooler is the birthplace of the Brothers Dalziell the celebrated engravers on wood. George was born in 1815, Edward in 1817, and John in 1822. Along with the more famous Thomas Bewick and Joseph Crawhall they played a part in the development of illustrated books.

Wooler Tower

On Tower Hill once stood the castle of the Muschamps, to whom the barony was granted by Henry I. It was probably a motte and bailey castle and no stone structure was erected here in the middle ages. Wooler was described in 1255 as having "a waste motte of no value".

However, by 1509, in a list of holds Wooler is described as a tower which would hold 20 horsemen. Probably this tower was built on the original mound as fragments of masonry still survive here. In 1526 it is described as new and in 1541 as a "lytle towre standyinge strongely, which dyd muche releyve as well the Inhabytants of the same towne as of two or three vyllages nere adjoyninge thereunto. Yt stode in a marvelous convenyent place for the defence of the countrye thereaboute, and the half of yt ys fallen downe for lacke of reparacons nowe lately this same yere. And yt had muche nede to be reedyfyed againe for the defence of all that quarter. And yt is thought that fourtye pounds would yett repare the ruynes and decayes thereof.

In 1545 its garrison formed part of the defences of the Border but by 1580 it was once again in need of repair. It was worse when in 1584 Christopher Dacre drew up his plans for the defence of the frontier but nothing seems to have been done. Hence the heap of rubble which is all that is left to-day.

In the immediate neighbourhood of Wooler are some objects of historical interest.

The Wishing or Pin Well. Just south of Wooler on the road to Earle is Horsdon Hill where the annual cattle and sheep fair used to be held. At its foot is the *Wishing Well.* A curious pagan custom was long observed here. On May Day a procession of people marched from Wooler to the well and each person dropped a crooked pin into it and wished their wish. Overhanging the well is a projecting rock called the *King's Chair.* It formerly bore a resemblance to a seat in which a king sat and directed a legendary battle in the plain below. This tract of land is called the "*Kettles*" which has given its name to a prehistoric camp (also called Maiden Castle or Greenside) which occupies the whole summit of the hill. It is quadrangular in shape, covering four acres. The place is called the Kettles from the many pot-like cavities to be found in the neighbourhood which are probably remains of prehistoric dwellings.

Whetting Stone. This is a large sandstone on which the inhabitants of Wooler are said to have sharpened their weapons in the period of Border warfare. It lies between Wooler Cottage and Burn House.

Cup and Saucer Camp. Half a mile from Wooler Market Place and south west of Humbleton Hill this prehistoric fortress crowns a conical hill. The rampart of stone and earth is still three feet high and is divided into two like a motte and bailey castle; hence the name of "cup and saucer".

EARLE

Formerly known as Yardhill it means "hill with an enclosure" and probably records a prehistoric camp. It stand on the road to Cheviot through Langleeford and is now merely two or three houses. Traces of ancient husbandry are numerous in the vicinity. The top of Earle Whin has been cultivated on the ridge and balk system. In 1541 we read that . . . *the towneshippe of Yerdle conteyneth x husbandlands and hath in yt a bastell house without a barmekyn and ys of thinherytaunce of Thomas Hepburne esqre. and Gylbert Scotte.* Nothing can be traced to show the site of this tower. Christopher Dacre's map of 1584 shows the tower with a note—"Here at Yerdle the east and mydell marche is divided"

Nearby is Middleton Hall. The commissioners of 1541 reported that "the towneshippe of Mydleton Hall centeyneth iiii husband lands plenyshed and hath in yt two stone houses or bastells the one of th' inheritance of Robt. Rotherforthe and thother of John Rotherforthe". No trace of them remains today but Middleton Hall probably occupies the site of one and Tomlinson said the foundations of the other could be seen in his day in an adjacent field.

HUMBLETON

At Humbleton, one mile north of Wooler, the medieval village which lay around a triangular village green, has disappeared. In 1296 it was a place of some importance and was assessed at £39. Only piles of stones and a few broken walls mark the spot which now lies within a circle of by-roads. The decline has been caused by the absorption of the small freeholders by the large landowners. To the west *Humbleton Hill* rises to a height of 977 feet. It is crowned with a prehistoric camp probably built shortly before the arrival of the Romans. A striking feature are the lynchets or cultivation terraces of which there are three successive tiers just below the ramparts. All around the lower slopes are remains of hut-circles, folds for cattle, and oval tombs. Beyond the hut circles a craggy ravine called Monday Cleugh separates Humbleton Hill from the great fortress of *Harehope Camp* built on a promontory the base of which is protected by an ancient wall. It is approached by a narrow carriageway bordered by earthern ramparts. The walls of the camp, composed of earth and stones, are almost complete. The entrance crosses the walls obliquely, and is protected by an inner guardhouse. There are only a few hut circles within the ramparts since the central area was intended mainly for the security of the cattle in times of alarm. The camp commands a wide view and stands in line with those on Humbleton Hill, Yeavering Bell, and Kettles Hill. This chain of hill forts is linked with a series of trackways to the south.

Beneath Humbleton Hill took place the famous Battle of Homildon Hill in 1402. The Earl of Douglas was returning home after laying waste much of Northumberland to the very walls of Newcastle when he was overtaken by the Earl of Northumberland and his son Henry Hotspur with George Dunbar, Earl of March who was Douglas' mortal enemy. The battle was won by the English archers who slaughtered 800 scotsmen on the field of battle. The wounded Douglas was taken prisoner along with many other knights and noblemen. The site of the battle is marked by a large upright stone which stands in a field called "Redriggs". It is called the *Bendor Stone* and a century ago the Bender Inn stood nearby.

FOWBERRY TOWER

Fowberry Tower lies two miles N.E. of Wooler. It was an oblong tower-house first mentioned in 1513. It was burnt by the Scots in 1541. Its owner Roger Fowberry, is described in 1595 as a "great theve". However his house was mortgaged to the Strother family who took possession and in 1666 rebuilt the medieval tower as a comfortable house. Further rebuilding took place in 1776 and nothing remains of the original building. The work was completed in 1809 by Matthew Culley who is famous in the history of Northumbrian agriculture. A quarter of a mile from Fowberry Hall is Castle Hill, but there is no evidence that this was the site of an early motte and bailey castle.

Inscription formerly on Doddington Bastle.

DODDINGTON BASTLE

Doddington is three miles from Wooler and is now a small village with a ruined tower in the centre. That it was once more important may be gathered from a tradition that on the occasion of a Doddington man dying at Belford, forty lairds of Doddington, each riding his own horse, went over to attend the funeral. The tower is now a ruin but at the end of the last century was well preserved with a red roof, as our illustration shows. It is an oblong bastle-house built in 1584 as the inscription, once on the tower, states. Since it was erected at a time when the border was settling down it was built as much for comfort as defence. Oblong in shape it had a projecting porch and staircase on the south. It is three storeyed and gabled with small square headed windows. The exterior measured 57 feet by 25 feet with walls 3 feet 6 inches thick. It had a ridged roof and embattled parapet on the north and south.

Doddington Bastle House.

YEAVERING

The Celts came to Northumberland about 600 B.C. The hill fort defended by stone-ramparts as at Yeavering, developed at a later date. The hills around Wooler were one of the main centres of population in pre-Roman Northumbria. Yeavering was the main stronghold of the whole area. Here a large community with over 130 timber huts occupied the summit of the hill, an area of 12 acres, forming the finest prehistoric camp in the north.

When in the late 6th and early 7th century the Ayles overrun Northumbria they established their royal town at Old Yeavering below the great Celtic fortress. It was here in 627 that the missionary Paulinius stayed at the royal palace of Edwin (583-633) and for thirty-six days baptised converts in the river Glen which is close by. Bede called the place *Ad Gefrin*. He says that the town was abandoned under the following kings and a new place built at *Melmin*, which some people have claimed is Millfield. Our drawing shows a reconstruction of this famous anglian town.

In a field between old and new Yeavering is a large upright stone, commemorating the battle of "Geteryne" (as the place was then called) when in 1415 Sir Robert Umfraville, called Robin-mend-the Market with an army of some 500 men defeated a party of 4,000 scots and chased them across the Border.

King Edwin's Royal Capital at Yeavering

KIRKNEWTON

The village of Kirknewton is in one of the most beautiful situations in Northumberland. It lies at the confluence of the River Glen and the College Burn. The scenery around is wild and hilly. To the south rises the Newton Tors (1,762 feet), to the south-east is Yeavering Bell (1,182 feet) while in the background lies Cheviot himself "Hill after hill, green with soft herbage on which sheep are grazing, or gaping with grey rocky fissures, and tufted with alpine plants and heather; deep gorges with burns rushing through them down to the glen, clouds passing and hiding hill-top after hill-top; moor grouse and solitary birds swooping now and then, are leading characteristics of this extensive and sparsely-inhabited district". Immediately above the village is Gregory's Hill the site of a small earthwork and close by is West Hill (703 feet) with another prehistoric enclosure containing the foundations of round dwellings. A village so close to the Border was bound to suffer the disastrous incursions of Scottish raiders.

KIRKNEWTON CHURCH

Northd

Published Feby 1824 by W. Davison Alnwick

Kirknewton Church

This is a remarkable building. It was rebuilt in the time of Charles II and restored under Dobson in 1860 and contains remnants of the original Norman edifice. The chancel—one of the most unusual in the country—has walls less than three feet high and from them rises a plain pointed vault. It is thought to be the vaulted chamber of a pele tower built out of the ruins of the Norman church. It is entered from the nave by a low and narrow segmental arch. Set in the wall beside the arch is a rough Norman sculpture representing the Adoration of the Magi. The Madonna and Child are shown seated in a sort of trough both with their arms raised. The Magi are shown running towards them with raised arms carrying gifts. They seem to be attired in kilts and are bare-footed.

At right angles to the chancel is a smaller but similar chamber, supposed to be an ancient chantry, now called the Burrell Vault. The font is panelled in lozenges and is dated 1663. Built into the outside wall of the tower is a child's coffin lid with a decorated floriated cross upon it. Set against the wall of the south chapel is a rare tombstone of 1458 with incised figures of Andrew Bowrell and his wife, in the churchyard Josephine Butler the famous social reformer lies buried. She was born at Millfield in 1828 the daughter of John Grey of Dilston a noted agrictultural reformer.

Kirknewton Tower

The tower here is firstmentioned in 1415. The commissioners in 1541 reported: "at Est Newton there ys a lytle towre and a stone house joyned to the same the walls of which stone house ys so lowe that in the last warres the Scotts wanne the said stone house and sett fyer on yt and had thereby allmost brunte the tower and all. The experyence whereof sheweth that yt were expedyente to rase the walls of the said stone house higher and to fortefye the same able for the defence of common skrymyshes".

However, in spite of the tower, the village was regularly raided and large numbers of cattle seized. One of the last attacks was made by 2,000 horsemen in 1570. They took 400 head of cattle, horses, mares and household gear, and 200 prisoners "besides the hurting of divers, women and the throwing of sucking children out of their clouts".

The tower was still in existence in 1584 but has now completely disappeared.

HETHPOOL

From Kirknewton a road runs south to Hethpool (O.S. Heath pool) a lonely hamlet of a few shepherd's cottages, but once a place of some importance. In the Subsidy Roll of 1296 no less than 18 people are assessed as owning chattels of a total value of £48 16s. 2d. The name signifies "pool under Great Hetha".

Heathpool House is a modern mansion built in 1919 on the site of a house erected in 1687, as an inscription over the door states. By the front gate are four guns. The inscription on one tells us that it "was one of the twelve cannons which in 1812 were mounted on top of the keep of the old castle at Newcastle upon Tyne to be fired on days of public rejoicings". In the garden stands the remains of Hethpool Pele. It is a ruin completely smothered in ivy standing to the height of two storeys with walls 4 feet thick. In the Middle Ages the area was regularly laid waste and the tower was described in 1541 as "a lytle stone house or pyle whiche ys a greate releyffe to the tenants thereof". The tower is very small and was clearly only used in times of emergency.

On Harrowbog one mile to the south is a wood of most curious, old, gnarled oaks, which belonged to Lord Collingwood. These he desired might never be cut down, because they would grow into such fine 'knee timber' for his ships."

The valley of the Colledge burn is rich in memorials of pre-historic times. The cultivation terraces which occur at Hethpool are remarkable. "Similar terraces", says Mr. Tate, are seen in the valley of the Breamish, but those on the Colledge are more marked, distinct and numerous. White Hill, near the farm-house is terraced to its summit with sixteen terraces."

KILHAM

The village of Kilham, the site of a border pele, now consists of scattered houses, It lies at the foot of Kilham Hill (1,108 feet) two miles north of Kirknewton. On the north side of the river is *Howsdon* hill of which the poet Story wrote. "It is remarkable as being the very first to acknowledge, by its verdue, the favours of returning spring. Its base, when I kept sheep upon it in my boyish days, used to exhibit a perfect forest of broom."

Describing the hills around he wrote:

> "These mountains wild, "began the maiden," claim,
> Each for itself, a separate local name.

We stand on *Lanton Hill.* Not far behind,
The verdant *Howsden* woos the summer wind.
That mountain, with its three wild peaks before,
Is styled by dwellers near it *Newton Torr.*
The oak-clad ridges there of *Akeld* swell,
And here the bolder slopes of *Yevering Bell.*
While towering yonder, with his patch of snow,
And proudly overlooking all below,
Is CHEVIOT's mighty self, his throne who fills,
The admitted Monarch of Northumbrian hills."

KILHAM TOWER

In 1890 Bates tells us that remains were still to be seen and the tower resembled the bastle-house at Doddington though on a smaller scale. This is the only real evidence that a fortress was ever built here. The Border Commissioners writing in 1541 tell us that "the townshippe of Kylham conteyneth XXVI husband lands nowe well plenyshed an hathe in yt nether tower barmekyn nor other fortresse whiche ys greatt petye for yt woulde susteyne many able men for defence of those borders yf yt had a tower and barmekyn buylded in yt where nowe yt lyeth waste in every warre and then yt is a greatt tyme after or yt can be replenyshed againe."

Lying close to the Border and on Bowmont Water the area was regularly laid waste so the need for a tower was great. Christopher Dacre's plan of 1584 shows such a fortification but, since the map probably showed the defences of the Border as they should be rather than as they were, this is no definite proof. In fact thirteen years later Sir Robert Carey reported to the Privy Council. "On the 14th instant at night four Scotsmen broke up a poor man's door at Kilham taking his cattle. The town followed, rescued the goods, sore hurt three of the Scots, and brought them back prisoners. The fourth Scot raised his country meanwhile, and at daybreak 40 horse and foot attacked Kilham, but being resisted by the town, who behaved themselves very honestly, they were driven off and two more were taken prisoners. Whereon the Scots raised Tyvidale, being near hand, and to the number of 160 horse and foot came back by seven in the morning, and not only rescued all the prisoners, but slew a man, left seven for dead and hurt very sore a great many other." A graphic account of the life lived on the Border in those days. No wonder towers and peles were needed.

PASTON

Two miles further to the west is the hamlet of Paston (Old English *Paelloe's farm*) which lies in a fertile valley in strong contrast to the bleak hills around. On Paston Hill (755 feet) is a large circular pre-historic camp with a small lake at its foot. Paston Hall is a pleasant modern building whose vaulted basement is part of the old tower.

MILFIELD

Six miles north east of Wooler is the pleasant village of Milfield. It is first mentioned in the 16th century and the association of the name with the *Melmin* of Bede is doubtful. In August 1512 a large Scottish raiding party under Alexander, Lord Home, was ambushed here by a much smaller English army under Sir William Bulmer and completely routed. This skirmish, a year before the battle of Flodden, "was the fyrst open token of warre shewed by the Scottes, which call this journey —the yll Roade."

Millfield Plain, the bed of the great Glendale Lake in pre-historic times, was used as a racecourse in the 18th century "A gold cup of sixty guineas value" was run for in 1723 and races were held as late as 1790. Part of Milfield became the property of the Grey family in the 18th century. When George Grey came here "the plain was still a forest of wild broom. He took his axe and, like a back wood settler, cut away the broom and cleared for himself a space on which to begin his farming functions." He died in 1793 and his son John became one of the great Northumbrian agriculturalists. He was a progressive man supporting Parliamentary Reform, the abolition of Slavery, and the repeal of the Corn Laws. In 1833 he took charge of the Greenwich Hospital estates and moved to Dilston. He was a great writer on all agricultural questions and maintained that for agriculture to become a science "the culture of the mind must precede that of the land."

RIVERS AND STREAMS

THE TILL

"In Till there's good store of fat trouts to be won,
Let your skill load your creel as you wander along,
And at night, as you tell of the feats you have done,
Cheer your talk with a cup of good wine and a song."

The Till is a continuation of the Breamish from the one arched Bewick Bridge near Bewick Mill, as the old rhyme says:

"The foot o' Breamish and the head o' Till,
Meet together at Bewick Mill."

It joins the Tweed at Tillmouth, near Twizell. It is a deep and slow-running river and can be very dangerous:

"*Says Tweed to Till,*
"*What gars ye rin sae still*?"

"Sae still as I rin, and sae fast as ye gae
Where ye drown ae man, a'll drown twae."

THE BREAMISH

This fine trout stream rises in the very heart of the Cheviot hills. It flows generally eastward until it reaches the neighbourhood of Powburn at which it turns north. The name is Celtic probably like the Welsh—*brefu*—to roar.

THE GLEN

This stream is formed by the junction of the College and Beaumont at Westnewton and joins the Till near Newtown. It gives its name to the valley called Glendale. A British river name meaning *clean, beautiful.*

THE BOWMONT

In the 13th century this stream was called Bolbent. The origin of its pre-English name is obscure. It drains the parishes of Morebattle and Yetholm before joining the College burn.

THE COLLEGE

The College is formed at Southern Knowe by the junction of two burns called the Fleehope and Lamsden, the former rising near Henhole the latter near the Bizzle. About two miles before joining the Beaumont it falls in a succession of cascades called Heathpool Linn.

THE WOOLER WATER

It rises near Scotsman's Knowe in the heart of the Cheviots. At first it is called the Harthope Burn (the section near Langleeford is sometimes called Langleeford burn). When it is joined by the Caer burn (formed from the Common and Hazelly burns) its name changes to Coldgate Water. At the Haugh Head it finally assumes the name of Wooler Water, entering the Till five miles further on.

Carved Rock at Rowting Lynn. George Tate, 1865.

FENTON

Fenton Town is a group of 19th century buildings, a self-contained Northumbrian farm, lying four miles north by west from Wooler. It has developed with the decline of the older Fenton Tower.

Fenton Tower

The tower is first mentioned in 1415 and was held by Ralph Grey. In 1509 it was inhabited by Christoffer Clapam and had accommodation for 40 men. The commissioners who surveyed the Border in 1541 described it as "a grett towre with a barmekyn in great decaye in the rooffe and floores and the walls of the barmekyn with other necessary houses within the same and yt were muche requysyte that yt were kepte in reparations for yt standeth in a very convenient and apte place for lyinge of an hundreth men in garryson in tyme of warre against Scotland." These repairs seem to have been carried out because next year along with Ford and Etal it is described as a "house of strengthe". In 1549 one hundred foot-men were stationed at Fenton under the command of Sir John Forster, and the tower was also used for the confinement of Scottish prisoners. We last hear of Felton tower in 1715 when John Warburton describes Fenton as a "village of 12 houses on the east side of the river Till, in which are the remains of an ancient tower". Remains of the tower could be seen in the farm house garden just over 100 years ago.

In its early days Fenton was the smallest parish in Northumberland. Nearby is Fenton Hall built by the Earl of Durham from 1871 to 1875. With its ornamental facade, tall tower, extensive grounds and artificial lake it is a pleasant house in a fine situation.

Two miles north of Fenton is *Rowting Linn* a pretty waterfall on the Broomride burn. It probably receives its name Rowting, a *bellowing* from the noise it makes in tumbling 30 feet over the sandstone cliffs. At *Fenton Hill* nearby are the remains of a prehistoric camp. The Kimmerston to Barmoor road crosses the glen and north of it is a prehistoric camp which has some fine rock carvings—the famous cup and ring markings—which are probably of religious significance.

CHILLINGHAM

Chillingham was one of the earliest of anglian settlements and like other similar communities a site was chosen on low ground near a river. Later a new settlement was added nearby called Chillingham Newtown which was sufficiently large that to the muster of 1579 it could supply eleven men equipped with horse and armour and eight others without equipment. It has now shrunk to a small farm hamlet. The pretty village of Chillingham itself has a fine church which was founded in the 13th century. Enclosed within the modern porch is a Norman doorway with cushioned capitals. Many of the large stones used in the 12th century nave are probably anglian in origin. The chancel and nave are Norman, the vaulted crypt is 16th century and the classical belfry was erected in 1753. Between 1829 and 1839 the

CHILLINGHAM CHURCH,
Northd.
Published Janʸ 1824. by W. Davison Alnwick.

church was restored and a great deal of the older part removed. There is a painting by John Varley which shows the church interior before these alterations were made.

The tall and slender octagonal stone font bears the following inscription:—

GOD BLIS THE CHV RCH M R.W ANNO DOM 1670

The fine oak cover with scalloped finial is probably contemporary. There is also a fine Jacobean oak pulpit, panelled and areaded but deprived of its ornate canopy in 1829 and reduced in height. In St. Mary's chapel is a Georgian fireplace and the magnificent Grey altar tomb. It is a sumptuous monument of great artistic importance and

is almost in its original condition except for the missing canopy or "tester" which once surmounted it. It was built about 1445 of sandstone with alabaster figures of Sir Ralph Grey and his wife. The sides of the tomb are richly decorated with fourteen figures of saints in niches separated by figures of angels. The background or reredos consists of a standing angel holding a crested helmet and in each side panel smaller angels flying to Heaven with a soul wrapped in a sheet. Above is a Jacobean addition with elaborate cartouche and obelisks. The alabaster figures are English but the pedestal was almost certainly imported. It has been suggested it might have been looted from Bishop's Kennedy's barge which was wrecked at Bamburgh when on a voyage to St. Andrew's.

In the churchyard is an 18th century headstone to Hugh Bowety the castle gardener. A crossed spade and rake on the back denote his trade.

THE HURLSTONE

On the top of a rounded hill to the south of Chillingham Newtown is a mysterious pillar called the Hurlstone. The name is probably a corruption of 'Earl's Stone' although some say it was given that name by people who believed in giants and explained that it had been *hurled*

The Hurlstone

there by one of their race. To confuse matters there is carved on one side the date 1838. Perhaps that is the date when it was moved to its present spot.

The following local tradition is related about this stone. From Vateran's Cave (once the resort of smugglers) on Bewick Moor to the Henhole on Cheviot there used to run a subterranean passage. Some people decided to explore this route. After hourneying three or four miles they had reached as far as the Hurlstone. Suddenly all their lights went out and they heard above the galloping of horses and strange voices crying:

> Hup! hup! and gee again!
> Round and round the Hurl Stane.

CHILLINGHAM CASTLE

As with many castles which have been extensively altered and where documentary evidence is lacking, the early history of Chillingham castle is obscure. In the 13th century a mansion house probably existed here since Henry III stayed here in 1255, and Edward I in 1298. Certain walls in the basement are thought to date from this period. In January 1344 Thomas de Heten was granted a licence to fortify his *mansum* (mansion-house) of Chevelyngham with a wall of lime and stone, to crenellate it, and to make it into a castle or fortalice. The work must have been completed by 1348 for in this year Sir Thomas de Heton granted the vicar a room above the castle gate and stabling for two horses in the west hall.

The castle then consisted of a courtyard with a tower at each corner, an entrance gate on the south, with the great hall on the east

Chillingham Castle from the N

THE WEST VIEW OF CHILLINGHAM-CASTLE, IN NORTHUMBERLAND.

To the Right Hon.ble CHARLES Earl of Tankervile; Lord Ossulston & Baron Ossulston in the County of Middlesex; Owner of this Castle. This Prospect is humbly Inscrib'd by Your Lordships most Obed.t Hum.ble Serv.ts Sam.l & Nath.l Buck.

THIS Castle was for many Ages ye Seat of the Chief of the Noble Family of ye Greys Barons of Wark, it is a Manor within the Barony of Woller, of old call'd the Barony of Muschamp, which Barony had also been long in the Possession of the said Noble Family which becoming extinct in the Person of Ralph late Baron of Wark, the same descended to the present Possessor in right of his Mother, who was the only Daughter of Ford Baron of Wark, and Earl of Tankervile.

Chillingham Park by T. A. Allom, 1832.

and various buildings on the west. The north wall was considered dangerous and left blank. William de Heton, the last of his family, died in 1400. Within a few years the Grays of Heton took over, the first owner being Sir Ralph Gray who died in 1443, and whose magnificent altar tomb is in the parish church. In 1509 the castle was reported as capable of accommodating 100 horsemen. Although during the Pilgrimage of Grace (1536) the castle was beseiged and probably damaged, it was reported in 1541 as being in a fair state. This period in the castle's history has left no visible remains apart from three carved heads above the fireplace in the "still room". They are supposed to represent Henry VIII and his queen. The Grays owned Chillingham till 1701 when on the death of Ford Gray, Earl of Tankerville the estate became the property of his only daughter Lady Ossulton whose husband later became the Earl of Tankerville.

Before their time however an extensive reconstruction of the castle was carried out. The main entrance was moved to the north wall where it is today and the south and north sides of the courtyard rebuilt. While this rebuilding was in progress the famous story of the toadstone occurred. Here is the account of 1695: "*In the Hall, at Chillingham Castle, there is a Chimneypiece with a hollow in the middle of it; wherein ('tis said) there was found a live Toad, at the Sawing of the Stone. The other part of it is also still to be seen (with the like mark upon it, and put to the same use) at Horton Castle*".

Inigo Jones is supposed to have been the architect who re-designed the castle at this time but there is no evidence to prove this. Today the castle consists of the four ancient towers (extensively altered), connected by later buildings which enclose a courtyard. On one side of this courtyard were cloisters approached by a fine stairway. The magnificent entrance is in the north. The grounds with their fine avenues of limes were laid out by Sir Jeffrey Wyatville in 1828. He carried out similar work at Windsor Castle.

In 1933 the contents of the castle were sold by auction and the building is now unoccupied.

THE CHILLINGHAM WILD CATTLE

In 1279 John de Vesci obtained a licence to enclose his moor at Chatton which lay within the royal forest. Whether the original "wild cattle" were in this park we do not know. In any case this park was destroyed before the 17th century. In 1629 William Lord Grey of Chillingham obtained a licence to enclose 1,500 acres in Chillingham and in 1634 the tenants of Chatton complained that in the enclosure part of Chatton Moor (called Robin Hood's Bog) had been taken. A few years later the wild cattle are mentioned for the first time. In January, 1645/6 one of Lord Grey's servants wrote to his master complaining about the Scots troops who had occupied the district:—

"*What with the Soldiers, and this continuing Storme if it lye but one Month more, there will bee neither Beast nor Sheepe left in the*

country. Your Honour's Deere and wild Cattle, I fear will all dye, doe what wee can: The lik of this storme hath not beene knowne by any living in the Country. The Lord looke uppon us in Mercy, if it be his blessed Will. "

After this there are a number of references to the cattle. In 1756 the Earl of Tankerville celebrated his son's birthday by ordering that "a great number of the wild cattle in Chillingham park to be slaughtered, which, with a proportionable quantity of bread, were on that day distributed among upwards of 600 poor people".

In his *British Quadrupeds* (1789) Thomas Bewick published an account of the cattle by John Bailey, the steward of the Earl of Tankerville. This account was re-published in the famous agricultural survey of John Bailey and George Culley called the *General View of the Agriculture of the county of Northumberland* (1797). This account is one of the best descriptions of the cattle and we here quote it in full.

Wood Engraving by Thomas Bewick

"Their colour is invariably white, muzzle black; the whole of the inside of the ear, and about one-third of the outside from the tip, downwards, red; horns white, with black tips, very fine, and bent upwards; some of the bulls have a thin upright mane, about an inch and a half, or two inches long; the weight of the oxen is from 35 to 45 stone; and the cows from 25 to 35 stone, the four quarters; 14 lbs. to the stone. The beef is finely marbled and of excellent flavour . . . The mode of killing them was, perhaps, the only modern remains of the grandeur of ancient hunting. On notice being given that a wild bull would be killed upon a certain day, the inhabitants of the neighbourhood came in great numbers, both horse and foot; the horsemen rode off the bull from the rest of the herd until he stood at bay, when a marksman dismounted and shot. At some of these huntings, twenty or thirty shots have been fired before he was subdued: on such occasions, the bleeding victim grew desperately furious, from the smarting of his wounds, and the shouts of savage joy that were echoing from every side. From the number of accidents that happened, this dangerous mode has been seldom practised of late years, the park-keeper alone generally shooting them with a rifled gun, at one shot.

When the cows calve, they hide their calves for a week or ten days, in some sequestered situation, and go and suckle them two or three times a day. If any persons come near the calves, they clap their heads close to the ground and lie like a hare in form to hide themselves . . . When any one of the cattle happens to be wounded, or grown weak and feeble through age or sickness, the rest of the herd set upon it and gore it to death.

The origin of the Chillingham Cattle is obscure. There is no evidence that they are descended from the Celtic Shorthorn which were the domestic herds of Neolithic times nor of the Scottish *Urus* which were once found in the Highlands. It has been suggested that they were brought over by the Anglo-Saxons and the white skinned cattle were for religious reasons separated and inbred. During troubled times some would escape and revert to their wild habits.

The herd is under the complete control of the "King" bull who is the only one to mate with the cows. He reigns supreme for two or three years until he is successfully challenged and defeated in combat. Like all inbred animals the cows are poor breeders and suckle their calves for very long periods which prevents the herd increasing rapidly. The cattle feed during the evening, mostly sleeping during the day. Their sense of smell is acute and if a calf is handled by a human being the other cows detect the smell and kill it. They eat nothing but grass, hay or straw and even if starving in the winter will not touch any other cattle feed. In the severe winter of 1947 the herd was nearly destroyed being reduced to thirteen animals. Probably the greatest danger now facing the herd is the possibility of foot and mouth disease breaking out in the neighbourhood.

The herd is now maintained by the Chillingham Wild Cattle Association, a non-profit making body which was formed in 1939.

CHEVIOT WILD GOATS

The Cheviots are famous for their wildlife. Henry Tegner in his book *Charm of the Cheviots* has covered this subject in great detail so there is no need to repeat his work. However the Cheviot wild goats are so famous that we would like to summarize his description: The wild goat is not a native of these islands and was probably brought here by the Phoenicians. Domestic goats were once of value to farmers but have been replaced by sheep. The wild goats we see today undoubtedly have escaped from domestic herds. How numerous they are on the Cheviots nobody knows but the severity of the terrain keeps their numbers down. Their herd instinct is very strong and unlike hill sheep they always keep together in a compact body. Writing in his book *Bird-Life of the Borders* Abel Chapman says: "It may be asked why animals yielding no return in fleece or flesh, are granted free pasture on the hills. The answer given by the shepherds is unanimous — "The goats earn their livelihood by killing adders".

THE DUDDO STONES

Northumberland is rich in prehistoric remains. It has the largest concentration of cup and ring marks to be found anywhere, prehistoric hill forts abound, and burial mounds are abundant. They show that the area was important in prehistoric times. However there are no remains to compare with Stonehenge or Avebury although isolated stones can be found. At Duddo however we can see the finest stone circle remaining in our county. Canon Raine in his history of North Durham (1852) described this prehistoric relic.

"On an eminence in the middle of a field north west of Duddo stands a time and weather worn memorial of the Druidical period. The temple, or whatever it may have been, has been of the usual circular shape, surrounding at intervals a plot of 36 feet in diameter. Four stones alone are standing, the tallest of which measures 6 feet 9 inches in height, by 13 feet in girth: a fifth is extended upon the ground, in a broken state; the rest have been removed. The remains of an outer circle were a while ago discovered at the usual distance. The situation of this hillock is of a peculiar nature· it rises, as it were, in the middle of a large natural basin two miles in diameter and might have been seen at one and the same time by thousands upon thousands of assembled devotees. A small barrow at the foot of the hill on the north side, much levelled by the plough, has I believe never been opened".

It must be noted that the stones at Duddo were erected long before the Druids and their purpose is still a matter of dispute.

FORD

Although it was the home of a prominent Border family and an important part of the defences of the Border. Ford did not play an important part in the history of Northumberland. When peace came to the Borders in the 16th century Ford was a small village whose interests were completely agricultural, with a market of its own. An

Grooved Monolith, Duddo.

anonymous 18th century document called "*Peculiar customs that prevail among the Common People of Ford*" records some of the traditional customs which still survived in the village.

On Shrove Tuesday the schoolboys as in other northern areas were "allowed to fight a cock upon paying the schoolmaster a penny". The owner of the victorious bird was called the "victor" and the runner-up was known as "the victor's man". On Palm Sunday the victor had "the honour of running from the church about a mile and back again attended by his man". He was pursued by the rest of the boys who carried palm rods. They were handicapped however by having to run round the church three times before starting. If he were overtaken the "victor" would be lucky "if he escapes a severe flogging, tho' his man, or second endeavours to ward off the blows as much as possible".

On Shrove Tuesday also took place a football match between the married and single but before the match began all who had been married during the past year had "to jump or wade through a wide deep watery hole which they call the gaudy loup". On Easter Tuesday "the Dow Dancing" took place. It started with mass dancing in the village street and they "two female contestants are singled out to dance with each other as long as then can". The winner was given a pigeon decorated with coloured ribands. It had been held up by the feet while the dancing contest was on. On Midsummer Eve a bonfire of horse's bone was lit on a neighbouring hill but this practice had recently fallen into disuse. All Saint's Eve, "commonly called Nutcrock Night", was the night when the young villagers stole cabbages from the gardens which they then threw down people's chimneys. This dangerous practice was widely prevalent at the time.

The parish church of St. Michael although much altered and restored by Dobson in 1853 is an old early 13th century building. The sturdy bell turret is of great interest. It is built on a broad heavy central buttress against the west wall like a chimney breast. Its pyramidal upper stage has window openings for the bells.

The village at Ford was built in the 19th century by Lady Waterford. The school is dated 1860. The school is decorated with a series of water-colours on paper which look like frescoes. They depict Biblical scenes using as models the village people. They are a great tourist attraction but to many people they make little impact. Ruskin thought little of them. "I expected", he wrote to her, "you would have done something better".

It is difficult to imagine coal mining at Ford but the mine was flourishing in the 17th century and continued working well into the present century.

The FORGE near FORD CASTLE

FORD FORGE

Ford Forge was built in 1769 and was once famous for the manufacture of spades. The buildings are restored. The print reproduced here shows the works in 1779.

Bedroom in Ford Castle
Where KING JAMES IV slept prior to The Battle of Flodden

NORTHUMBERLAND FARE by Margaret Slack. £1.20.
This is a little gem of a recipe book but also a fascinating essay on social history. We are treated to the *original* versions of recipes for such delights as singin' hinnies, leek pudding and pan haggerty, and the more aristocratic Duke of Northumberland Cake. But author Margaret Slack is not only a cook but a social historian. She gives a fascinating glimpse into the lives of working and upper class families of the last century, including their basic diets and weekly food budgets.

THE LIFE OF BILLY PURVIS. The Famous Geordie Comedian. 1875. Facsimile. £2.50.
"Billy Purvis (1784-1853) was the most famous clown and jester the north has ever known. His acting became a legend in lands between the Tees and Tweed. His life is not only the story of a great actor and comedian but also a social history of the area. In it we meet a way of life, methods of entertainment and an industrial and rural society which has now passed away." The first life of the great clown called *Life and Adventures of Billy Purvis* was written by J. P. Robson and published in 1849. Other editions followed. The present biography was published by T. Arthur in 1875.

FORD FORGE c. 1920

FORD SMITHY

The old smithy at Ford is an extremely picturesque building as our illustration shows. The great horseshoe round the door is carved in stone.

FORD CASTLE, 1887.

FORD CASTLE

Although not actually on the border like Wark, Norham and Berwick, Ford played an important part in its defence. The castle was originally built by William Heron, who obtained a licence to crenellate his manor house in 1338. By 1367 it was reckoned as an important fortress in the defence of the Border and was one of those supervised by Henry Percy le Fitz who at the time controlled the key castles on the frontier. But in 1385 Ford was taken by the Scots and dismantled. A few years later is was described as a ruined castle. By 1509 the castle was either restored or rebuilt and was occupied by William Selby. In 1513 James IV crossed the border and seized the castles ot Etal and Ford and before the battle of Flodden set them on fire. The Border Survey of 1541 informs us that although the castle was partially restored following the Scottish defeat most of the buildings remained in ruins. However a few years later Ford successfully resisted

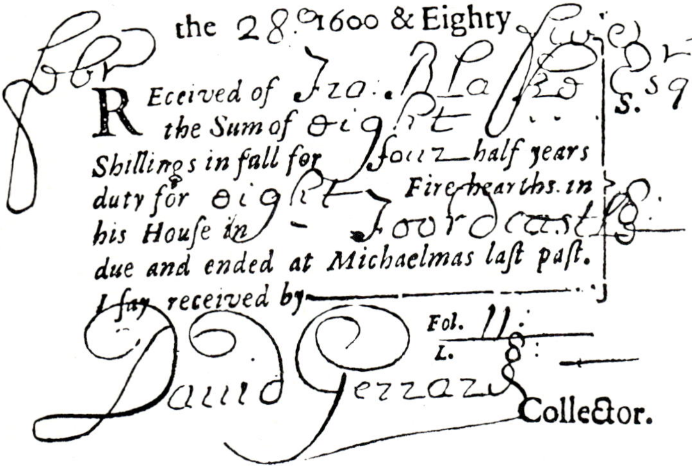
Febr the 28. 1600 & Eighty five
Received of Jno: Blake Esq:
the Sum of eight s.
Shillings in full for foure half years
duty for eight Fire-hearths in
his House in Foordcastle
due and ended at Michaelmas last past.
I say received by
Fol. 11
L. 8
David Gerrard Collector.

RECEIPT FOR HEARTH MONEY IN 1685 FOR FORD CASTLE.

a strong attack by French troops who were fighting on behalf of the Scots. All the castle was wrecked apart from one tower in which Thomas Carr held out. No repairs were carried out and Ford ceased to be a border fortress. The Scots were back again in 1640 during the Civil War and we are told "they deal very subtilly, they hurt no man and pay for what they take, so the country gives them all the assistance they can. Many of the country gentry come to them and entertain them, one of them in Mr. Carr of Ford". However when eight years later the royalists came to Ford their behaviour was quite different. It was plundered and everything of value taken away.

The male line of the Carrs of Ford ended about 1667 and by various heiresses the castle passed through the families of Blake of Delaval to the Marquis of Waterford in 1822.

By permission of Bodlean Library

This drawing is probably by the Bucks about 1728. *It shows the walls of the east and west wings facing the courtyard. The room above the hall is marked "Chaple" with pointed windows. Over the door are arms of Acron quartering Muschamp with initials W.C. In the gable of porch are the arms of Blake with date* 1677 *under initials F.B.E. On vane of S.E. tower are words "Sr F.B.* 1695".

meet him at Newcastle. With an army of 30,000 to 40,000 men he advanced to Alnwick, Bolton and then to Wooler haugh. From here the English challenged the Scottish army to come down into the plain of Millfield to do battle. Finding the Scots were unwilling to give up their strong position Surrey marched to Barmoor Wood, four miles from Flodden.

Meanwhile many of the Scottish contingent had decided to return home so when the battle took place the armies were almost equal in numbers. However, the English army was in poor condition. During their march north the weather had been very wet. Worse still "there was little or no wine, ale, nor beer for the people to be refreshed with but all the army for the most part were enforced and constrained of necessity to drink water". The Scottish army, on the contrary, was well provisioned and had been resting for several days.

Early in the morning of the 9th Surrey left his camp and with his vanguard crossed the bridge at Twizel while the rearguard crossed at the ford near Heton Castle. The scene is thus described by Sir Walter Scott.

"From Flodden ridge
The Scots beheld the English host
Leave Barmoor Wood, their evening post
And heedful watched them as they crossed
The Till by Twizel Bridge.
High sight it is, and haughty, while
They dive into the deep defile;
Beneath the caverned cliff they fall,
Beneath the castle's airy wall.
By rock, by oak, by hawthorn tree,
Troop after troop are disappearing;
Troop after troop their banners rearing,
Upon the eastern bank you see.
Still pouring down the rocky glen,
Where flows the sullen Till,
And rising from the dim-wood glen,
Standards on standards, men on men,
In slow procession still,
And sweeiping o'er the Gothic arch,
And pressing on in ceaseless march,
To gain the opposing hill."

James has often been accused of military incapacity because he failed to attack the English as they were crossing the Till. But there were strong reasons why he should maintain his strong position at Flodden. To the north of Branxton was a large swamp which the Scots thought would be a serious obstacle for the English army. However part of the English forces skirted the moss and the remainder crossed by "Branx Bridge" a crossing unknown to the Scots. Realising that the enemy were making for Branxton Hill, which was as strong a position as Flodden and would cut off his escape into Scotland, James ordered the camp refuse to be set on fire and taking advantage of the dense smoke which a south-easterly breeze blew over the whole ridge, he transferred his forces to Branxton ridge. The plan of the battle shows the disposition of the forces.

The battle started with an artillery duel. As soon as the Scottish guns opened fire the men of Tynemouth and Bamburghshire, who were in Dacre's rearguard, fled, followed by Edmund Cheshire's followers who resented not being led by a Stanley. The English artillery was, however, superior and used more effectively.

The struggle was soon conducted at close quarters. The left wing of the Scots under the Earl of Huntley and Lord Home, "with long spears like Moorish pikes" put the English right wing, under Sir Edmund Howard, to fllight. But the Scottish advance was halted by a band of north-countrymen led by John Heron, the bastard. The Scots under Crawford and Errol then engaged the Lord-Admiral and the English were soon in a serious position. The Scottish centre, led by James himself, and Surrey were then locked in combat and for a while the Scots were in the ascendant.

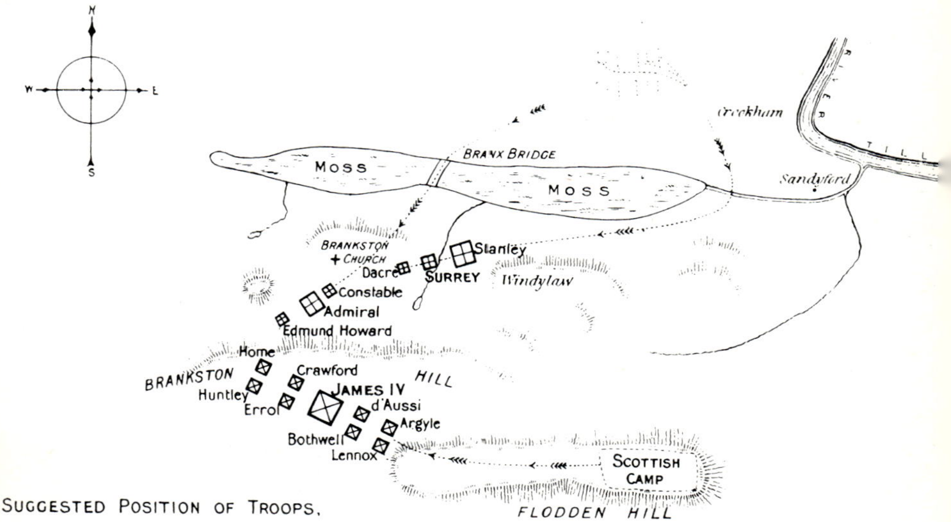

SUGGESTED POSITION OF TROOPS,
AT COMMENCEMENT OF
BATTLE OF FLODDEN.

The battle was, however, decided on the English left wing which was attacked by half naked highlanders under Lennox and Argyle. The English archers here wreaked havoc upon the clansmen and then advanced with the pikemen to the top of the ridge. Attacking the Scottish centre in the rear, a dreadful slaughter took place. The king and thirty of his noblemen were slain. The scene is described by Sir Walter Scott:

"The English shafts in volleys hail'd:
In headlong charge their horse assailed;
Front, flank, and rear, their squadrons sweep
To break the Scottish circle deep,
That fought around their king.
But yet, though thick the shafts as snow,
Though charging knights like whirlwinds go,
Though bill-men ply the ghastly blow,
  Unbroken was the ring;
The stubborn spearmen still make good
Their dark impenetrable wood,
Each stepping where his comrade stood,
  The instant that he fell.
No thought was there of dastard flight;
Link'd in the serried phalanx tight,
Groom fought like noble, squire like knight,
  As fearlessly and well.
Till utter darkness closed her wing
O'er their thin host and wounded king.

At the crisis of battle Lord Home refused to come to the king's assistance saying, "He does well that does for himself. We have foughten our vanguards, and have won the same, therefore let the lame do their part as well as we." Then joined by the moss-troopers of Tynedale and Teviotdale his men stripped the slain and plundered the baggage of *both* armies.

Fighting on a small scale continued next day until the rest of the Scottish army learnt of the death of their king. Among the booty captured by the English were seven beautiful cannon from Edinburgh Castle, called "The Seven Sisters".

THE HISTORY OF NEWCASTLE *upon* TYNE:

OR, THE ANCIENT *and* PRESENT STATE OF THAT TOWN.

By the late *HENRY BOURNE*, M. A.
Curate of ALL-HALLOWS in NEWCASTLE.

——*Hæc* —— *alias inter Caput extulit Urbes* ——VIRG. Ecl. I.

NEWCASTLE upon *TYNE*:
Printed and Sold by JOHN WHITE. M.DCC.XXXVI.